PRETTY FABULOUS

FASHION AND CRAFT
ACTIVITY BOOK

ARCTURUS

ARCTURUS

This edition published in 2014 by Arcturus Publishing Limited
26/27 Bickels Yard, 151–153 Bermondsey Street,
London SE1 3HA

Crafts and photography by Annalise Lim
Illustrated by Katy Jackson
Designed by Elaine Wilkinson
Written by Annalise Lim and Penny Worms
Edited by Kate Overy, Joe Harris and Sara Gerlings

ISBN: 978-1-78212-599-0
CH003794NT
Supplier 26, Date 0414, Print Run 2891

Printed in China

Contents

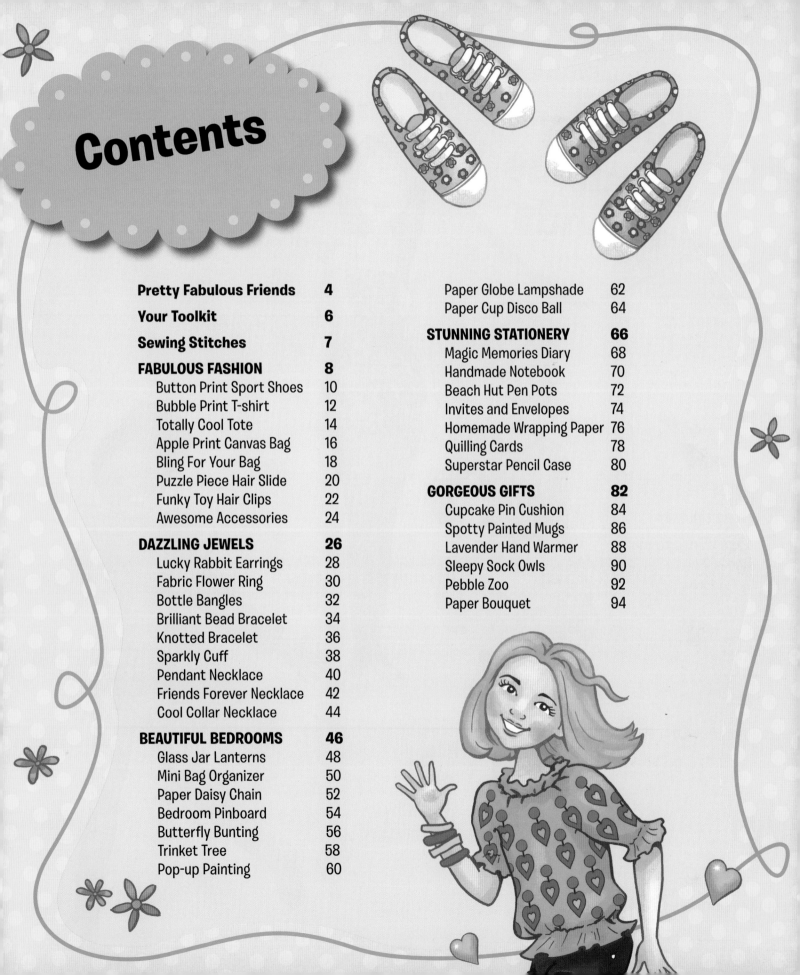

Pretty Fabulous Friends

Meet the Pretty Fabulous Friends.
They are all creative and love
making gorgeous things.

Kimberly
Loves: animals

Style tip: animal prints

Fave thing to make:
anything animal related

Alexa
Loves: bags

Style tip: wear pink

Fave things to make:
accessories

Mia
Loves: having fun!

Style tip: keep it green

Fave thing to make:
something from nothing

Sasha

Loves: adventure

Style tip: keep it simple!

Fave thing to make: something for her room

Chloe

Loves: hats and hairbands

Style tip: stay on-trend

Fave things to make: gifts for friends

Lily

Loves: shoes

Style tip: recycle your fashion!

Fave things to make: customized clothes

5

Your Toolkit

Paint and brushes

Paint is essential for most crafts, and a selection of brushes will help too. Synthetic brushes work especially well. Special fabric paint is sometimes needed for fabulous fashion items.

Scissors and craft knives

Make sure you have a good pair of scissors, but be careful when you use them! If you need to cut tougher materials like plastic, ask an adult to help. NEVER use a craft knife on your own. Your fingers are precious!

Knickknacks

You will soon realize that you can make many things out of lots of household items. Collect little knickknacks that might make interesting crafting items, such as buttons, bubble wrap, tiny toys, and corks.

Glue

You'll need the right glue for the job. PVA or white glue works well for sticking paper or wood. Fabric glue is essential for sticking fabric to fabric, paper, or cardboard. Use craft glue for sticking plastic or shiny things. Super glue is super strong, but never use this on your own.

Needle and thread

Sewing is a fashion essential, so you'll need a sharp needle with a large enough eye for you to pass thread through. Ask an adult to help you the first time you use a needle, so that you don't prick yourself. You are shown what to do in the book.

Felt and fabric

Fabric frays and felt does not. Most of the time, you will want to avoid leaving a raw (unstitched) fabric edge, as your project will not last as long. Felt is easy to cut and you can either stick it together with fabric glue or sew it together with a needle and thread.

Sewing Stitches

Before you start you might need to learn a few basic stitches!

Tacking stitch

This stitch is used to temporarily hold two pieces of fabric together. It is then removed when you have finished your neat stitches. Make sure you have put a knot in the thread and make long, loose stitches that go in and out of the fabric.

Running stitch

First tie a knot in your thread, then sew two small stitches on top of each other. Make sure that each stitch and the gap between the stitches are the same length. To finish, tie a knot in the thread at the back of the fabric before you cut off the unused part of the thread with scissors.

Back stitch

Make your first stitch the same as you would a running stitch. Push the needle up through the fabric, but instead of moving it forward to make the next stitch, push it back through the same hole as the previous stitch you made and back up again so you are in front of the stitch. Repeat this along the fabric.

(For blanket or whip stitch see page 14)

Fabulous Fashion

The Pretty Fabulous Friends love to customize their clothes to make them unique. In this chapter, they're sharing some of their best fashion tips and secrets.

Customize, personalize

You can adapt all the craft activities in this book to something that is totally you. Choose the ones that work best for you and adapt the design for a unique look that no one else can copy.

Keep it clean

Getting messy is all in a day's work for a crafter. Always lay newspaper or plastic over the surface you're working on and have a damp cloth close to hand for any small spills or splatters.

Button Print Sports Shoes

Give plain sports shoes a makeover. Using a magical blend of buttons, corks, and fabric paint, you can transform plain shoes into something fresh and fabulous. Sporty Sasha just loves them!

You will need:

★ Bottle corks
★ Buttons
★ Craft glue
★ Canvas sports shoes
★ Fabric paint
★ Paintbrush
★ Black felt-tip pen

So Cool!

1

Glue some buttons on to the tops of the corks using craft glue. Leave them to dry.

2

Use a paintbrush to paint a layer of fabric paint on to one of the button stamps.

3

Press the stamp on to the shoe and lift it off to reveal your print. Repeat with all the other button stamps and cover your shoes with lots of prints.

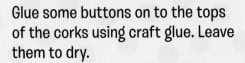

4

Add to your design using a black felt-tip pen.

5

Paint the laces with a bright fabric paint and leave them to dry before you relace your shoes.

Now you're ready to put them on and strut your stuff!

Bubble Print T-shirt

Don't pop it, print it! Bubble wrap makes fun spotty prints. Kimberly has made a heart print that is so on-trend. You can make one for your friend using a different pattern!

You will need:

* ★ Bubble wrap
* ★ Scissors
* ★ Fabric paint
* ★ Plain T-shirt
* ★ Plastic chopping board
* ★ Paintbrush

1

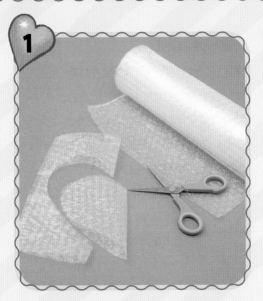

Fold a piece of bubble wrap in half and cut out a teardrop shape, as shown above. When you unfold it, it will make a heart.

2

Paint a thin layer of red paint on to a flat surface such as a plastic chopping board.

3

Add some more paints to the palette, using a paintbrush.

4

Lie the bubble wrap face down in the paint. Press it down firmly.

5

Transfer the bubble wrap on to your T-shirt and press it down firmly again. Gently lift up the bubble wrap to reveal the print! Print the heart using a contrasting shade of paint. Leave to dry.

Totally Cool Tote

Appliqué is the craft of sewing decorations on to material. It can make something ordinary look totally original. Decorate a canvas tote using this technique and you will really stand out from the crowd. Lily has gone for a tortoise design! It's totally cute!

You will need:

* Plain canvas bag
* Fabric in different shades
* Needle and thread
* Ribbon
* Pins
* Pen and paper
* Scissors
* Felt

Blanket or whip stitch

These stitches are used to sew two pieces of fabric together.
A whip stitch is pretty simple. Loop the thread around and around in a spiral, passing it through the fabric. A blanket stitch (shown here) is a little harder. Sew even stitches as shown, starting at least 1 cm (0.4 in) from the edge, making sure you pass the needle through the loop you make with each stitch, as if you are making a row of right angles.

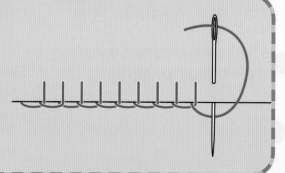

1

Draw a design on to a piece of paper using a marker pen. Lily has drawn a tortoise shape. Cut it out with scissors. This is your template.

2

Pin your paper template on to your fabric and cut it out. Repeat this four more times using a variety of different fabrics.

3

Sew four fabric shapes on to the bottom of the bag using a needle and thread. A whip stitch or blanket stitch will work nicely. Space them out as evenly as possible.

4

Sew the last fabric shape on to a piece of felt and cut around it, leaving a 1 cm (0.4 in) border of felt.

5

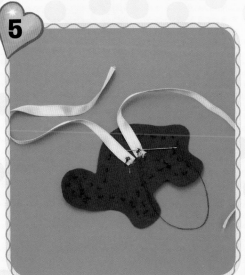

Sew two lengths of ribbon to the back of the felt shape. Tie it on to the handle of your canvas bag.

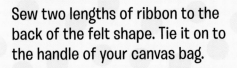

Apple Print Canvas Bag

Printing with fruit and vegetables is surprisingly easy and looks great. This fruity canvas bag is perfect for shopping trips. And no more plastic bags means it's good for the environment, so Mia thinks this bag rocks!

You will need:

★ Blank canvas bag
★ Apples
★ Fabric paint and paintbrush
★ Table knife
★ Plastic chopping board

It would make a great beach bag too!

1

Cut two apples in half. You may want to ask an adult to help.

2

Brush a thin layer of fabric paint on to a plastic chopping board.

3

Press the flat part of one apple on to the paint, making sure that the whole flat surface of the apple is covered.

4

Press the apple firmly on to the canvas bag and lift off to reveal the print.

5

Use another shade of paint, and repeat with the other apple until you have covered the whole bag.

Bling For Your Bag

Who doesn't like a bit of bling? Especially if it costs nothing! This button bling can be attached to a handle, purse, or loop. Pick out some jazzy buttons and beads.

You will need:

- ⋆ Beads
- ⋆ Buttons
- ⋆ Wire
- ⋆ Wire cutters
- ⋆ Keyring clasp

1

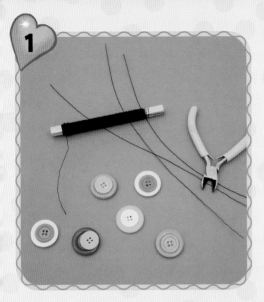

Arrange your buttons in a cross pattern, with some piled on top of each other. Make sure your base buttons are all the same size.

2

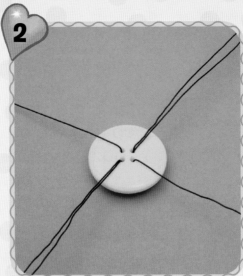

Cut a 30 cm (12 in) length of wire and start threading on the buttons from the horizontal part of the cross.

3

Cut another 30 cm (12 in) length of wire and thread the vertical buttons to make the cross.

4

Bend up the wires and twist them to fix them in place. Thread the beads up the twisted wires and make a wire loop at the top.

5

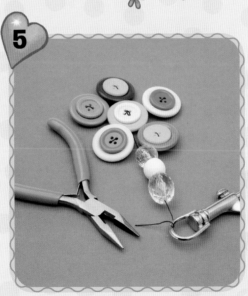

Attach the keyring clasp to the wire loop.

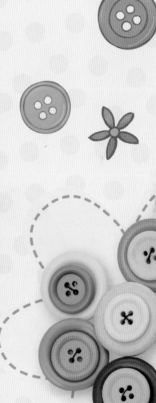

Puzzle Piece Hair Slide

Everyone knows that hair slides look great in long or short hair. These hair slides may look puzzling but they are so easy to make. You could start a puzzle craze by making them for your friends.

You will need:

* ★ Old puzzle pieces
* ★ Acrylic paint
* ★ Plain hair slide
* ★ Ribbon
* ★ Craft glue
* ★ Needle
* ★ Thread

1

Choose three old puzzle pieces that fit together in a row.

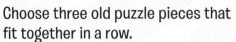

2

We've painted these puzzle pieces in blue and red.

3

Cut a length of ribbon and then fold it back on itself, securing the pleat with a stitch. Continue to pleat the ribbon at different angles to make it into a flower shape.

4

Use craft glue to stick the puzzle pieces on to the ribbon pleats.

5

Stick the puzzle pieces and ribbon on to the hair slide with the craft glue.

Funky Toy Hair Clips

This is the perfect craft for you if you have pieces of broken bric-a-brac or toys at home. Before you throw away these items, try revamping them into totally original and cool hair clips. Lily has made one for every outfit!

You will need:

* ★ Broken bric-a-brac or toys
* ★ Small beads
* ★ Plain hair clip
* ★ Super glue (never use this on your own)
* ★ Acrylic paint
* ★ Paintbrush
* ★ PVA glue

1

Collect together three items you want to attach to your clips and clean them so they are free of dirt and dust.

2

When they are completely dry, paint each one using your acrylic paints.

3

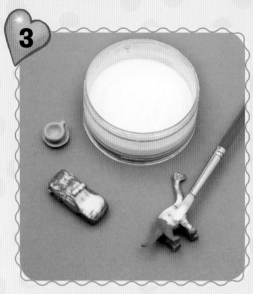

Cover the toys with a thin layer of PVA glue. This will protect the paintwork and give it a shiny finish.

4

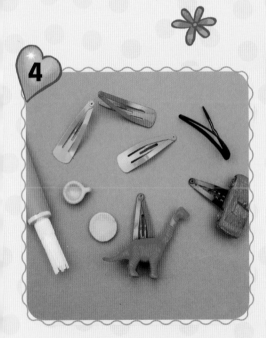

Ask an adult to superglue each toy to a clip and leave to set.

5

Now ask them to superglue some small beads on to the clips too.

Awesome Accessories

In Winter the Pretty Fabulous Friends wrap up with gloves, scarves, and hats and they have found a great way to decorate them with ribbon flowers. Why not try it?

You will need:

- ★ Ribbon
- ★ Buttons
- ★ Needle and thread
- ★ Scarf, gloves, and hat
- ★ Scissors
- ★ Tape measure

1

Cut a piece of ribbon to a length of 30 cm (12 in).

2

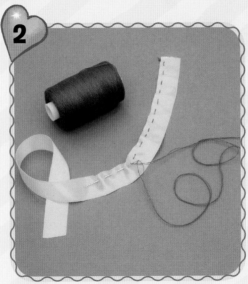

Sew a loose running stitch along one side of the ribbon, near the edge, leaving the needle still attached.

3

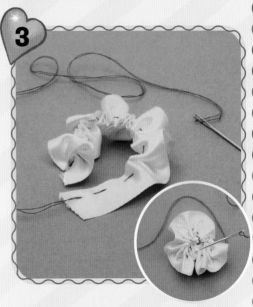

Pull the stitches tight, while ruching (frilling) the ribbon. Curl the ruched ribbon into a circle and secure it in place with a couple of stitches.

4

Make lots more of these flowers using different ribbons.

5

Sew them on to your gloves and scarf by placing a button into the middle of the flower. Stitch in place.

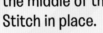

Dazzling Jewels

The Pretty Fabulous Friends like to stand out from the crowd with their handmade accessories. Here are their top tips for a totally unique look so you too can look a million dollars, while saving a fortune! All the crafts are easy to follow, but that doesn't mean your final pieces won't make a big impact.

Everyday treasures

You don't have to go shopping for craft material before getting started. First, look at what you have at home. You may have odd buttons from old clothes, a broken bead necklace, or a spare ribbon.

Shop around

Try looking in hardware stores for round washers, rings, or hooks, or secondhand stores for cheap accessories that you can recycle.

Keep it clean!

If you buy secondhand earrings, it's important that you clean them very thoroughly before wearing them. Ask an adult to soak them in boiling water for a few minutes and then disinfect them for you.

Lucky Rabbit Earrings

These earrings were created by Kimberly, inspired by her pet rabbit, Betty. Don't worry if you don't have your ears pierced. You can replace the hooks with clips.

You will need:

* Silver craft wire
* Small beads
* Felt
* Small pom-poms
* Scissors
* Fabric glue
* Earring hooks or clips
* Wire cutters

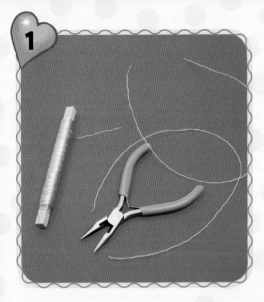

1

Cut two lengths of wire that are both 40 cm (16 in) long.

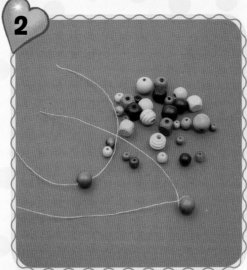

2

Place one medium-sized bead in the middle of the wire and twist once to hold it in place. This will be the rabbit's head.

3

Thread two small beads on to each of the wires and twist together with one twist. Poke both wire ends through a large bead (body) and then put another two beads (feet) on to the two wire ends. Twist in place.

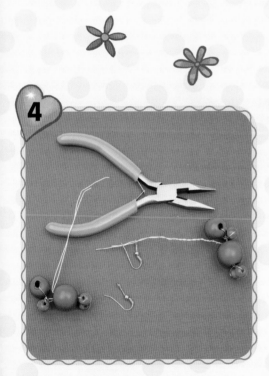

4

Poke the wires back through the bead body. Use the leftover wire to attach the earring hook or clip.

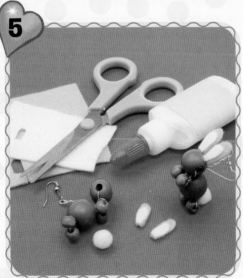

5

Cut out two felt ears and eyes, and stick it to the rabbit's head. Glue a small pom-pom to the back. Repeat all steps to make the second earring to make your pair.

Fabric Flower Ring

Alexa knows that rings, large or small, can really make an outfit complete. You can make lots in different styles to match different outfit choices, or just have one for every day of the week.

You will need:

* Felt
* An old ring
* Craft glue
* Fabric glue
* A button
* Needle and thread

1

Take two different pieces of felt. Cut out five petal shapes from one felt piece and five slightly smaller petal shapes from the other.

2

Pinch together the bottom of one petal and sew together using an overlapping stitch. Repeat this for all nine remaining petals.

3

Stitch the five larger petals together in the middle. Do the same with the five smaller petals.

4

Glue the two sets of petals together in the middle using your fabric glue. Leave to dry.

5

Use the craft glue to fix a big button to the middle of the flower. Leave to dry.

6

Sew the flower to your old ring.

Bottle Bangles

Chloe and Kimberly are always looking for ways to make gorgeous things from junk. Their latest idea is to make cool bracelets from old plastic bottles. These bangles look anything but trash!

You will need:

★ Large plastic bottle
★ Wool
★ Metallic embroidery thread
★ Clear tape
★ Scissors
★ Black marker pen
★ Ruler

1

Draw lines around a plastic bottle with a marker pen. Use a ruler to measure them. They should be around 3 cm (1 in) apart.

2

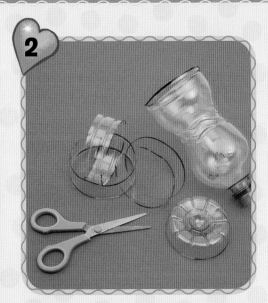

Cut along the lines to make plastic rings. These will be your bracelets!

3

Tape over the edges of each bracelet with some tape, so it is not sharp.

4

Wrap wool around and around each plastic bracelet. Use different shades of wool to make contrasting stripes. Then make a knot.

5

As a finishing touch, wind some metallic embroidery thread around each bracelet in a zigzag.

Brilliant Bead Bracelet

Sasha and Chloe have been having fun making their own beads and turning them into different bracelets and necklaces. Here's how to make Chloe's bracelet, but Sasha's necklace is just as easy.

You will need:

★ Polymer clay
★ Elastic
★ Clay tools
★ Wooden toothpick

1

Take three different pieces of polymer clay and warm them in your hands to make them soft.

2

By rolling the three pieces together into a large ball you will create a beautiful, marbled effect.

3

Break off pieces and roll into small round beads. You will need about 10 to 12 beads in total but make enough so they will fit around your wrist. Make a hole in each of the beads using the toothpick.

4

Make a small butterfly out of another piece of polymer clay using your clay tools. Stick this to one of your beads. Bake all of your polymer clay pieces in the oven as directed on the packet.

5

Once the clay has cooled down assemble the beads together on to a piece of elastic, knotting them in place.

Knotted Bracelet

Sailor's knots are useful to know if you are sailing the open seas, but did you ever think about using them to make a fashion bracelet? Chloe's figure-eight knotty bracelet looks chic but take your time so you don't get yourself tangled!

You will need:

* ★ String or rope 40 cm (16 in) long
* ★ Clasp and chain
* ★ Needle and thread
* ★ Beads

1

Place your rope down in front you with 20 cm (8 in) laid out. Bend the rest of the rope back on itself to make a loop.

2

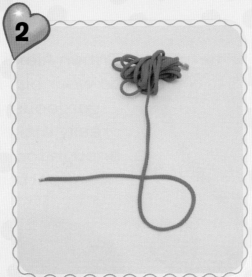

Take the rope up to make a letter "b" shape.

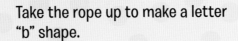

3

Bring the rope back down, but this time lead the rope behind the straight line. This will make your "8" shape.

4

Pass the rope through the bottom part of the "8" you have made and pull tight.

5

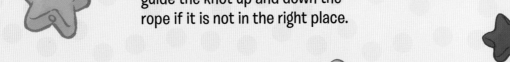

Repeat all along the rope until you have knotted the whole length, adding a bead at the bottom of every new knot. You can always guide the knot up and down the rope if it is not in the right place.

6

Measure the knotted rope against your wrist and trim as necessary. Then use your needle and thread to attach your clasp to each end.

Sparkly Cuff

When Alexa dresses up, she likes to wear big, bold accessories. This gorgeously glamorous cuff will really make an impact. It is large enough for you to create your own patterns and designs.

You will need:

★ Cardboard tube
★ Card
★ Scissors
★ Paint
★ Stick-on jewels
★ Craft glue
★ Metallic paint

1

Cut a 6 cm (2.5 in) length from your cardboard tube. Then cut a slice through it so that you can get the cuff on and off your wrist.

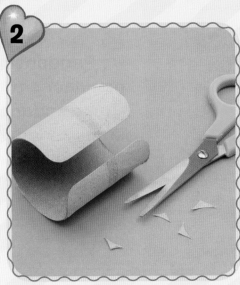

2

Round the edges of each corner using your scissors.

3

Decorate the cuff with card shapes and stick down with the craft glue.

4

Paint the whole cuff with metallic paint and leave to dry.

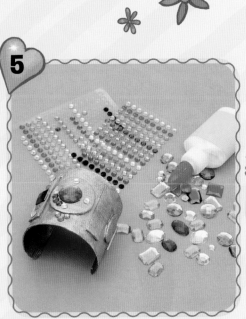

5

Decorate your cuff with some stick-on gems.

Pendant Necklace

Pendant necklaces are long necklaces that hang from a chain. The pendants can be as big or as small as you like. This one is made from simple metal washers, as elegantly modelled by Mia.

You will need:

* ★ Embroidery thread
* ★ Metal washers
* ★ An old chain

1

Tie a piece of embroidery thread around a small metal washer and start wrapping the thread around. Keep wrapping the thread until you have covered the whole washer. Repeat this two more times.

2

Tie the three small washers together with more embroidery thread so that they form a small triangle.

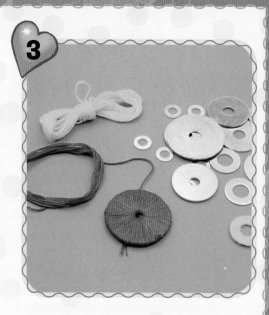

3

Wrap a large washer and a medium-sized washer with embroidery thread as in step 1.

4

Attach the small washer triangle to the large washer using more embroidery thread. Then attach the medium-sized washer to the bottom.

5

Thread your chain through the hole in the top washer.

Friends Forever Necklace

These two nearly identical bird necklaces are a perfect gift to give to a friend. You keep one and your friend has the other to remind you both of the great fun and laughs you have together. Lily has made them for herself and Sasha.

You will need:

* Leather thread
* Silver foil
* Cardboard
* Two hooks
* Craft glue
* Glitter glue

1

Cut out two matching pairs of birds from your cardboard. Make sure the pairs are slightly different from each other.

2

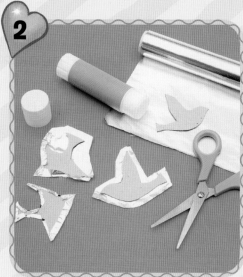

Cut out a slightly bigger version of the bird shapes with silver foil. Stick them on, then tuck the edges under.

3

Place a hook in the middle of each pair of birds. Glue the pairs together and leave to dry.

4

Add details to your birds with glitter glue. Leave to dry.

5

Add a leather thread to each of the hooks.

You could make this design too.

Cool Collar Necklace

Collar necklaces are so on-trend at the moment, and fashionistas Mia and Lily have come up with a way to make their own. They make an ordinary neckline into something extraordinary. You could add sequins and jewels if you like.

You will need:

* ★ Cardboard
* ★ PVA glue
* ★ Paint
* ★ Hole punch
* ★ Chain
* ★ Collage material
* ★ Pen or pencil

1

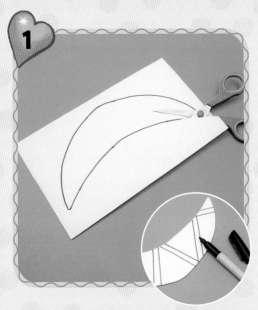

Cut out a crescent shape from your cardboard. Draw simple shapes into your cardboard collar.

2

Rip up your collage material into small shapes.

3

Using the PVA glue, start by gluing your collage material inside your main design.

4

Next, choose more collage material and glue it on to your collar. Coat the whole thing with a layer of PVA glue and leave to dry.

5

Punch a hole either side and thread the collar onto your chain.

Beautiful Bedrooms

Give your bedroom a makeover with these Pretty Fabulous craft ideas. Your room says a lot about you, but you don't have to go shopping to fill it with cool things. Just by being clever and creative, you can transform unwanted household items into amazing things.

What a load of junk!

Your home is sure to be full of unwanted objects that could be used in craft projects. Plastic containers are always handy. Scrap paper can be used in many different ways. You could cut up old clothes for textile crafts. Your friends and family will be amazed when you tell them your new craft projects are mostly made from junk!

Going global

By turning old things into beautiful things, you will not only save money but you will help the planet by keeping them out of landfill sites!

Glass Jar Lanterns

You can easily turn glass jars into beautiful lanterns to make a bedroom feel really cosy. The more you make, the better they will look when it gets dark! The perfect scene-setter for a Pretty Fabulous game of Truth or Dare!

You will need:

* ★ Glass jar
* ★ Tissue paper
* ★ Wire
* ★ Wire cutters
* ★ Buttons
* ★ PVA glue and brush
* ★ Tea light or LED light

Warning

Never light the candle yourself. Ask an adult to do it for you.

Also, the wire handle will get hot when the candle is lit, so don't touch it. Blow out the candle and leave the jar to cool before touching it.

1

Make sure your glass jar is clean. Coat the outside of the jar with a layer of PVA glue.

2

Tear up your tissue paper into small pieces and cover the outside of the jar with a layer of tissue paper. We have used pale blue.

3

Use scissors to cut out petal shapes from your tissue paper. Choose bright shades that will stand out from your blue base layer.

4

Coat your jar with a layer of PVA glue. Stick the tissue leaves on top. Then coat the whole jar in another layer of glue, and let it dry.

5

Ask an adult to cut a 50 cm (20 in) piece of wire and curl the ends so they aren't sharp. Wind it around the top of the jar to make a handle.

6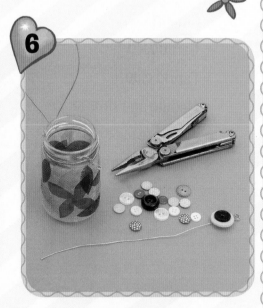

You will need adult help for this step too. Cut a 15 cm (6 in) piece of wire and thread a few buttons onto it. Attach it to the wire handle and twist the ends again. Finally, put a tea light or LED light inside the jar.

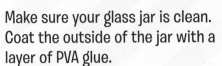

Mini Bag Organizer

Never lose little things again by keeping them in these handy mini storage bags, which look great hanging on any bedroom wall. They are perfect for keeping your hair accessories tidy and safe.

You will need:

* ★ Cotton fabric
* ★ Ribbon
* ★ Cardboard
* ★ Fabric glue
* ★ Needle and thread
* ★ Scissors
* ★ Tape measure

You could also make bigger bags for your sports or ballet gear.

1

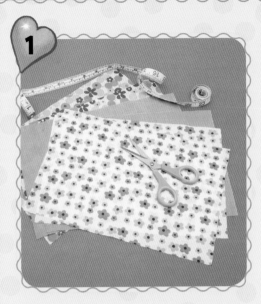
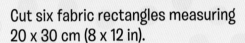

Cut six fabric rectangles measuring 20 x 30 cm (8 x 12 in).

2

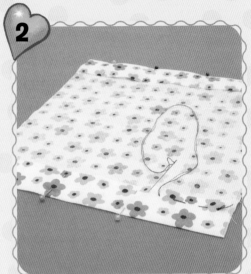

Fold the short sides of each rectangle over by 3 cm (1 in). Sew the folded edges in place with a back stitch. (See p.7)

3

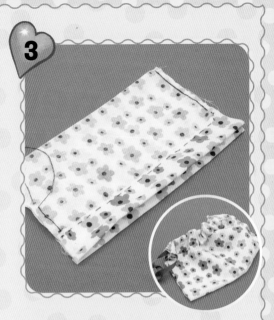

Fold each rectangle in half, with the outside of the cloth facing in. Sew up the two sides with a back stitch. Snip a "V" shape on either side and pass your drawstring ribbon through the holes. Repeat this five times.

4

Cut out a rectangle of cardboard measuring 50 x 40 cm (20 x 16 in). Then cut out a rectangle of fabric measuring 60 x 50 cm (24 x 20 in). Fold the edges of the fabric around the card and glue them in place.

5

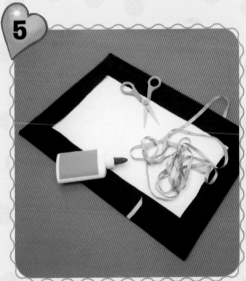

Cut two pieces of ribbon 50 cm (20 in) long. Wrap them around the cardboard and glue the ends down. Attach the mini bags to the ribbon (see right).

Paper Daisy Chain

Rescue some paper from the recycling box, and you can make a daisy chain that lasts forever! Hang it over your mirror or wrap it around the headboard of your bed for a pretty decoration. If you don't have a shredder, just use scissors.

You will need:

★ Shredder or scissors
★ Ruler and pen
★ Scrap paper
★ PVA glue
★ Green string

1

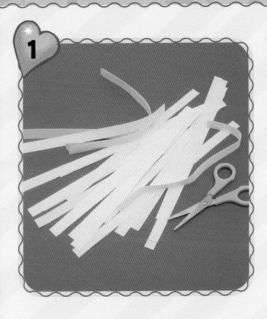

Either shred some white and yellow paper, or use a ruler, pen, and scissors to cut it into long strips. You will need 10 strips of yellow paper and 60 strips of white paper.

2

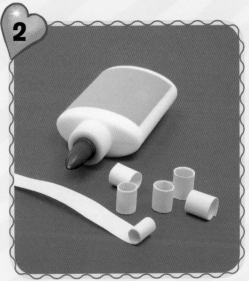

Coil the yellow paper into tight rings. Stick the ends in place with some PVA glue so they don't uncoil.

3

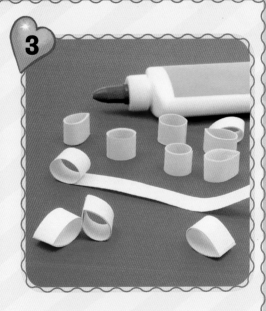

Coil up the white paper into slightly larger rings. Stick the ends in place with some glue. Pinch one end of each white ring to make a point. These will make your petals.

4

Stick six white petals to each yellow ring with PVA glue. Leave them to dry on a protected surface.

5

Now thread the flowers on to a length of green string.

You can create a variety of flowers using shredded magazines. Try decorating picture frames, blank cards, or even a keepsake box.

Bedroom Pinboard

If, like Chloe, you are always losing little notes, photos, and cards, what you need is a personalized pinboard to keep them all in one place! It's simple to make but looks great.

You will need:

* ★ Cardboard and paper
* ★ Marker pen
* ★ Ribbon
* ★ Fabric
* ★ Buttons
* ★ Fabric glue
* ★ Large plate

1

Draw around a large plate on to your cardboard. Then cut out the circle.

2

Cover the cardboard circle with some fabric. Cut the fabric a little larger than the plate and stick down the edge with fabric glue.

3

Cut six lengths of ribbon at least 5 cm (2 in) longer than your circle's diameter. Lay them over the fabric in a crisscross pattern. Turn over the circle, and glue the ends in place on the back.

4

Make a loop of ribbon and glue it to the back of the board, near the edge. Then draw around your plate on to a piece of paper.

5

Glue the paper on to the back of your board.

6

Glue some buttons on the front of your board where the ribbons cross over.

Butterfly Bunting

Kimberly adores pretty butterflies, and she has come up with this nature-inspired decoration to brighten up her room. The pattern is made by rubbing leaves and then adding paints.

You will need:

* Leaves
* Glue stick
* White paper
* Crayons
* Paints
* Craft glue or clear tape
* Ribbon
* Scissors
* Paintbrushes

1

Take two large leaves and two small ones. Stick them face-down on to a piece of paper using a glue stick, so that the raised veins are face-up.

2

Lay another piece of paper on top of the stuck-down leaves. Use the side of the crayon to make a rubbing of the leaf pattern.

3

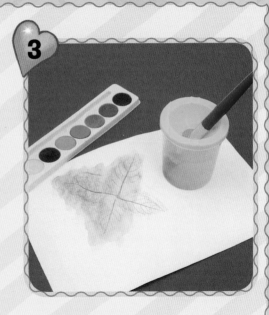

Paint a thin, watery layer of paint over the top of the rubbing. Leave the print to dry.

4

Cut around the leaf shape so it looks like a butterfly. Repeat steps 1 to 4 to make lots of different butterflies.

5

Stick the butterflies on to a length of ribbon using craft glue or clear tape.

6

To make the butterflies' bodies, cut them out of craft paper and stick them on with glue.

Trinket Tree

Is your dressing table as messy as Alexa's? She has lots of trinkets and hair accessories but she has nowhere to store them safely. The solution is to keep it tidy and show it off at the same time with this great trinket display tree!

You will need:

* Wire
* Metallic paint
* Cardboard
* Wire cutters
* Masking tape

1

Cut a 6 cm x 12 cm (2.5 in x 5 in) base from the cardboard.

2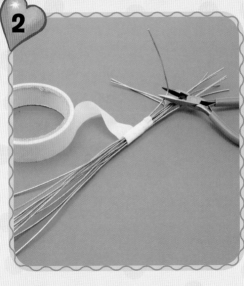

Cut ten 30 cm (12 in) lengths of wire using your wire cutters. Gather the wire together in a bunch and secure it in place with some masking tape.

3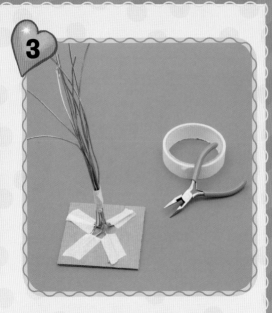

Spread out the wires at one end and secure to the base with masking tape. Spread out the top wires so that it makes the branches of your tree. Curl the ends using your wire cutters.

4

Cover the whole thing with masking tape, including the base. Leave to dry in a warm place.

5

Paint the tree in metallic paint and leave to dry before you hang your trinkets onto the tree.

Pop-up Painting

Paintings don't have to be flat. Mia's butterfly painting is a three-dimensional masterpiece that literally pops from the wall. You can use this technique to make cards too.

You will need:

* Canvas or thick cardboard
* Acrylic paint
* Paintbrush
* Craft paper
* Craft glue
* Scissors
* Pencil

1

With a brush, paint your canvas using acrylic paint. We've chosen bright pink.

2

Fold a piece of paper in half, and then in half again. Draw a large butterfly shape and a small butterfly shape on to one side and cut out using your scissors. This will make eight butterflies in total.

3

Fold a piece of green paper in half and half again. Draw some leaf shapes on to it and cut them out. Fold each butterfly and leaf in half so that it looks as if the butterflies are fluttering and the leaves are shaped like real leaves.

4

Start building up your canvas by gluing the leaves on to the canvas. Only glue down the folded edge so that the paper stands out from the canvas.

5

Glue the butterflies on in the same way. For a finishing touch, you could add some flowers. Make the petals like the leaves in step 3, but instead of folding them, curl them around a pencil.

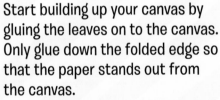

Paper Globe Lampshade

Sasha's room is her sanctuary. It's where she goes for some peace and quiet. She has used her creativity to add personal touches to unexciting furniture, including transforming a boring old lampshade into a pretty focal point.

You will need:

* ★ A paper globe lampshade
* ★ Tissue paper
* ★ PVA glue
* ★ Scissors
* ★ Pen
* ★ Paper

1

Draw a design on to a piece of paper. This pattern will be repeated around your lampshade three times.

2

Trace your design several times on to pieces of tissue paper. Copy different elements on to different sheets of tissue paper.

3

Cut out all your pieces using scissors and arrange them in order so they match your design. Cut enough pieces for three patterns.

4

Paint a thin layer of PVA glue on to the whole of the lampshade. Start sticking on your tissue paper designs, one piece at a time.

5

Coat the whole lampshade in another thin layer of PVA glue to seal the tissue paper in place.

Paper Cup Disco Ball

Disco balls are covered in mirrors that reflect light, adding a touch of glamour to any room. This decoration can do the same for your bedroom! Watch as the light bounces around when the sun hits it, or just add disco lights to create an immediate party atmosphere.

You will need:

★ 18 paper cups
★ Stapler
★ Mirrored cardboard
★ String
★ Glue stick
★ Scissors

1

Cut the bottoms off eighteen paper cups.

2

Stick a ring of eight paper cup rims together using a stapler.

3

Staple three more cups together in a line and then staple them to opposite cups in the ring to make a kind of bridge.

4

Staple two more cups to join the middle cup of the bridge and the middle cup on each side of the ring. Repeat steps 3 and 4 on the other side so that you make a complete globe.

5

Cut strips of mirrored cardboard and glue them to the inside of the cups.

6

Tie a piece of string to the top of your disco ball so you can hang it up.

Stunning Stationery

According to the Pretty Fabulous girls, there are two great things about going back to school. Firstly, seeing your friends, and secondly getting cool new stationery! Here are a few ideas to make your desk or school bag the envy of your friends.

Making the ordinary EXTRAordinary

You can customize just about anything! All the crafts in this section turn basic materials into something special. So don't throw things out when you can revamp, renew, and revitalize!

Keep it clean

If you are painting or using a messy technique, make sure you cover the surface you are working on with newspaper or a piece of plastic.

Magic Memories Diary

Transform a blank book into a summer diary in which you can share your memories, stick photos, and keep a friendship diary. Not only will the cover make it look special, it will protect it from sunscreen smears and ice-cream drips!

You will need:

* ★ Felt
* ★ Buttons
* ★ Ribbon
* ★ Felt glue
* ★ Needle and thread
* ★ Hardback book
* ★ Tape measure
* ★ Scissors

1

Open up your book and measure it. Cut a piece of felt 1 cm (0.4 in) taller and 6 cm (2.4 in) wider than the open book.

2

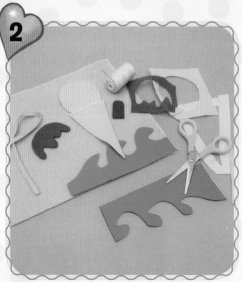

Cut out some felt shapes. For this design, you will need a pink circle, a yellow triangle, a blue wave, a little brown rectangle, and a red blobby shape (look at the picture!). Sew them in place with a running stitch. (See p.7)

3

Sew on some sequins. Stitch a button about 6 cm (2.4 in) from the right-hand edge.

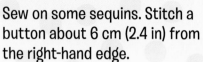

4

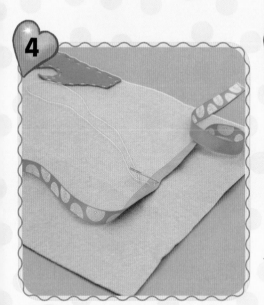

Cut a 20 cm (8 in) length of ribbon. Stitch it to the middle of the opposite side of the cover from the button, about 6 cm (2.4 in) from the edge. Attach it at the middle of the ribbon.

5

Fold over 3 cm (1 in) of each side. Sew a running stitch at the top and bottom of the folds. Slip the book inside the cover. Tie the ribbon to secure the book together.

Handmade Notebook

Sasha likes to be different so she doesn't just cover her notebooks with pretty paper, she makes the actual notebook herself from scratch! That way, she can put in different types of paper and create her own cover.

You will need:

- ★ 10 sheets of lettersize paper
- ★ Cardboard that is larger than the lettersize paper
- ★ A piece of wrapping paper that is slightly larger than the cardboard
- ★ Ribbon
- ★ Paper
- ★ Stapler
- ★ Glue stick
- ★ Clear tape

1

Fold the 10 pieces of paper in half and secure them in place by using one staple in the middle of the folded edge.

2

Cover one side of the cardboard with wrapping paper. Fold the paper around the edges of the card, and stick it down with tape.

3

Lay a length of ribbon on to the cardboard and fix it in place with the clear tape.

4

Cover the ribbon with a piece of paper that is slightly smaller than the card and fix it in place with a glue stick.

5

Fold the cardboard in half and sandwich the paper pages inside. Secure everything in place using two staples at the top and bottom of the spine.

6

To cover up the staples, we've stuck a piece of bright green paper along the spine.

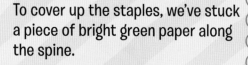

Beach Hut Pen Pots

The girls love spending time at the beach over the summer. With this craft, they can still be reminded of those sunny days even when the rain starts to pour. So why not bring a little sunshine into your room, while keeping things tidy at the same time?

You will need:

★ 2 kitchen roll tubes
★ Cardboard
★ Patterned paper
★ Cardboard
★ Sandpaper
★ Black marker pen
★ PVA glue
★ Scissors and ruler

1

Cut a piece of cardboard that measures 6 x 20 cm (2.5 x 8 in).

2

Cut some sandpaper to the same size as your cardboard and use PVA glue to stick it down.

3

Cut each kitchen roll tube in half, to make four tubes. Measure their height and cut four pieces of patterned paper to that height. Wrap the patterned paper around the tubes. Then stick it in place with PVA glue.

4

Cut four rectangles of cardboard measuring 8 x 3 cm (3 x 1 in). Fold them in half and cut a small notch into that fold. Fold the edge of the cardboard to the same depth as the notch. Cut four smaller 8 x 6 cm (3 x 2 in) rectangles. Draw on a dot.

5

Glue the card shapes to your tubes with PVA, as shown above. The pointed shapes are roofs, and the rectangles are doors. Glue the beach huts in a row on top of your sandpaper. Leave everything to dry.

Invites and Envelopes

The Pretty Fabulous Friends always make their own party invitations and their own envelopes to send them in too. Personalized stationery is a real treat to send, and even better to receive, so here's how to make your own.

You will need:

★ Wrapping paper
★ Plain paper
★ White label stickers
★ Glue stick
★ Scissors

1

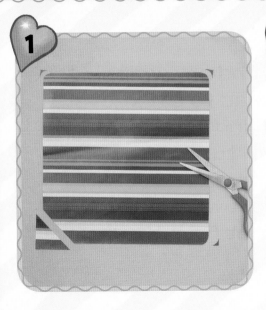

Cut a piece of wrapping paper into a square 20 cm x 20 cm (8 in x 8 in). Cut around three of the edges to make them round. Snip a triangle off the other corner.

2

Fold the flat corner into the middle on the other side of the paper. Press it firmly to make a crisp crease.

3

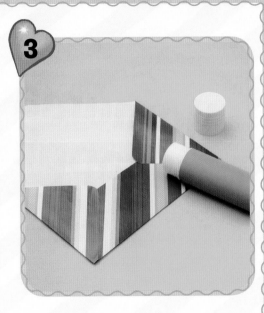

Fold in the two rounded corners on either side. Glue them in place with the glue stick.

4

Fold the last rounded corner in but do not stick it down.

5

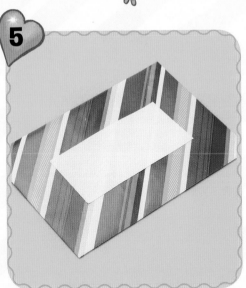

Turn over the envelope and stick a white label on to it.

6

For your letter, decorate a piece of plain paper with patterns cut from the wrapping paper you used to make the envelope.

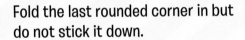

Homemade Wrapping Paper

If you can't find any wrapping paper then head to the kitchen. Here, you'll find some useful things that will turn white paper into ritzy wrapping paper. It's fun to make and it will make your gifts stand out from the rest!

You will need:

* Plain white or brown paper
* Plastic chopping board
* Plastic food wrap
* Silver foil
* Paper and scissors
* Poster paint and silver paint
* Paintbrush

1

Take three poster paints and spread them on to your chopping board, swirling them together with your paintbrush to make a pattern.

2

Lay a square of plastic wrap on to the paint mixture you have made and press it down.

3

Lift it off the paint and place it on to your paper. You don't want a flat print so it doesn't matter if it scrunches up. Peel off the plastic wrap to reveal your pattern.

4

Repeat steps 2 to 4 until you have covered the whole piece of paper. Leave to dry.

5

Now paint the chopping board with silver paint. Scrunch up some silver foil and press it onto the silver paint. Then place it on to the wrapping paper. You could add some glitter and ribbon to make your gifts look extra special.

Quilling Cards

Quilling is a way of folding or curling paper to create amazing patterns. Here's an idea for making birthday or thank you cards that are pretty to look at and easy to make. All you need is a steady hand!

You will need:

* Card
* A shredder
* Sheets of paper
* Scissors
* Glue stick
* Pen

1

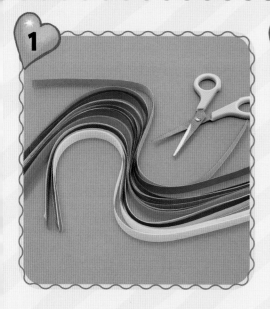

Use a shredder to cut the sheets of paper into strips. If you don't have a shredder you can always cut it by hand using scissors, but make sure the strips are as even as possible.

2

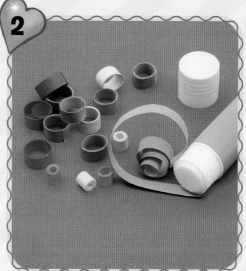

Coil each strip of paper into a tight circle and stick it in place using a glue stick.

3

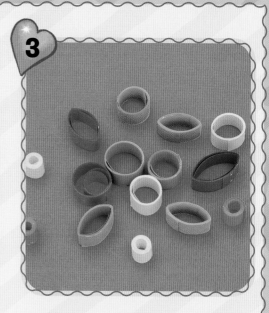

Make some of the circles big, and some of them small. Squash some of the circles so that they turn into ellipse shapes (as above).

4

Fold a piece of cardboard in two. Using a pen, draw a big star shape on one side.

5

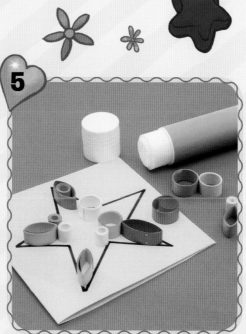

Cover the inside of the star shape with some glue stick and press the shapes into the glue. Fill the whole shape with the quilled coils of paper. Leave to dry.

Superstar Pencil Case

Sandpaper is not something normally associated with cool craft projects, but Kimberly has discovered that it's great for making one-off prints on to fabric. This customized pencil case is an important part of her back-to-school plans.

You will need:

* ★ Medium coarse sandpaper
* ★ Crayons
* ★ Iron
* ★ A plain fabric pencil case
* ★ Cardboard
* ★ Piece of fabric
* ★ Scissors

1

Cut a piece of sandpaper to the same shape as the pencil case. Then use the crayons to draw some pretty star shapes.

2

Keep adding to your picture to fill the whole space. Make sure that you press down firmly, to create a thick layer of wax.

3

Place a piece of cardboard beneath the fabric that you are going to transfer the pattern on to. We've placed it inside the pencil case.

4

Place your sandpaper on to your fabric with the pattern facing down. Cover it with the fabric.

5

Ask an adult to iron on top of the sandpaper for two to three minutes. Then lift it off to reveal the pattern on your pencil case!

Gorgeous Gifts

Giving gifts is a lovely thing to do. But giving gifts you've made yourself always feels extra special. It's not only easier than you think to make gorgeous things, it's also fun. And the time and effort you take over your handmade gifts will be appreciated for years to come by those who receive them.

Foraging Fun

It's possible to use natural objects in art and crafts all year round: from fresh flowers in your garden to pebbles from the beach. You can also forage for old socks in your sock drawer!

Careful as you sew

Make sure you ask an adult to help you with your first sewing projects, and always remember to be careful with sharp pins and needles.

Cupcake Pin Cusion

Chloe's grandma is always sewing, so Chloe has made her these cute cupcake pin cushions. They look delicious enough to eat, and are a great gift for anyone who is keen on handicrafts. They would also look good as decorations for someone's bedroom.

You will need:

* ★ Silicone cupcake liners
* ★ Cushion filling
* ★ Felt
* ★ Beads
* ★ Fabric glue
* ★ Needle and thread
* ★ Scissors
* ★ Ruler
* ★ Compass and pencil

1

Cut out a circle of felt that is 15 cm (6 in) in diameter. You can measure the circle with a ruler and compass.

2

Cut out the "frosting" with wiggly edges to the approximate size shown. Stitch using running stitch.

3

Sew some shiny beads to the wiggly felt shape with your needle and thread.

4

Sew a running stitch all around the edge of the felt circle. Leave the needle and thread still attached.

5

Gather the running stitch slowly so that you start to make a pouch.

6

Roll some cushion filling in your hands so it makes a ball. Place it in the felt pouch, then pull the running stitch tightly together, and sew the fabric closed. Glue the felt ball into the silicone liner and leave it to dry.

Spotty Painted Mugs

Chloe thinks there is nothing better than personalized presents. And here's one she's made for animal-loving Kimberly. Why not make one yourself? But beware, when you have a mug that looks this good, everyone will want to use it!

You will need:

* Ceramic paints
* Plain mug
* Carbon paper
* Paper
* Pencil
* Scissors
* Masking tape
* Cotton swab

1

Measure around your mug, then measure the height and cut a piece of paper to the same size. This is where you can design your mug.

2

Tape some carbon paper on to the mug, and then tape your design on top of that.

3

Trace over your design with a pencil, pressing hard. Then remove the paper from the mug to reveal a faint print.

4

Start to paint on the mug by dabbing on ceramic paint with a cotton swab.

5

Keep dotting on the ceramic paint until you have finished your picture! Then you will need to follow the instructions on the label of your ceramic paint to make it set. Most ceramic paints will need to be baked in the oven.

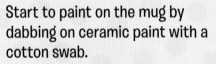

Warning

If the instructions for the ceramic paint tell you to use the oven, ask an adult to help. Don't do this on your own!

Lavender Hand Warmer

Lavender is one of the nicest smells of summer. You can collect the petals and dry them out to make into stuffing for these heart-shaped strawberries. Warm them up and they turn into winter warmers for chilly hands. Cosy!

You will need:

★ Red and green cotton fabric
★ Rice and cup
★ Dried lavender
★ Large cup or bowl
★ Scissors
★ Needle and white thread
★ Black marker

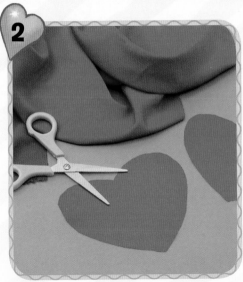

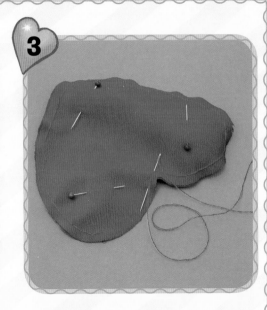

Fill a large cup or bowl two thirds of the way up with rice, then fill it to the top with dried lavender. Mix them together.

Cut out a heart shape from red fabric measuring about 12 cm (4.7 in) across. Trace around it with a marker, then cut out another identical shape.

Carefully sew the two hearts together around the edge, making sure you leave a small 5 cm (2 in) gap somewhere.

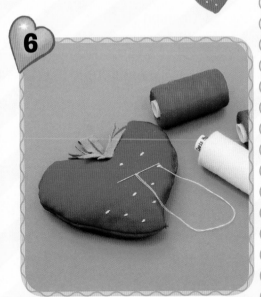

Cut out two stalk shapes and sew them onto each side of the strawberry. Sew on white seed shapes using your white cotton thread. Do this on both sides.

Turn the heart inside out to hide the stitching. Fill it with the rice mixture. Then sew up the gap to make sure nothing spills out.

Now put the bag into the microwave for 10 seconds to warm it up. The smell of lavender is very relaxing and the warmth can help to relieve aches and pains.

Sleepy Sock Owls

Mia has found something awesome to do with her odd socks. Turn them into lovable owls and give them to friends. She's even made a family of owls for her room. They are a hoot!

You will need:

★ Socks
★ Cushion stuffing
★ Felt
★ Needle and thread
★ Buttons
★ Scissors

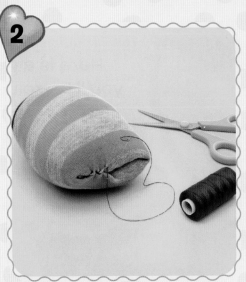

Choose an old sock and pack it with cushion stuffing until it is half full.

Tuck in the spare part of the sock and sew a few whip stitches to hold it in place. Tie a knot and snip off the loose end of the thread.

Using scissors, cut these shapes from felt: a large triangle for the face, two small triangles for the beak, two wings, two circles for eyes, two feet, and two feather shapes.

Sew all the felt shapes (except the beak) to your sock, using your needle and thread and a whip stitch.

Sew on the two small triangles to form the beak. Only sew on the short end of each triangle, so that the beak stands out from the face.

Use fabric glue to stick on some buttons for eyes. Glue a small button (the pupil) on top of a medium-sized button (the eye).

Pebble Zoo

Here is a gift idea that is so cute, you'll be reluctant to give them awa... This pebble zoo can b... used as paperweight... bookends, play pieces for games, or fun ornaments... Your friends will love them!

You will need:

★ Stones of different sizes
★ Craft glue
★ Fabric glue
★ Acrylic paint
★ Paintbrush
★ Felt
★ Scissors
★ Googly eyes
★ Black marker pen

tick a medium-sized stone to a
arge stone using craft glue, to
make a head and body for your
creature. Then glue four smaller
stones to the large stone to make
some legs.

Repeat step 1 twice. To make the
zebra, stick another small stone on
to the front of the medium stone.
This will be the muzzle.

Now, paint your pebble animals
using the acrylic paints.

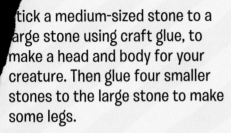

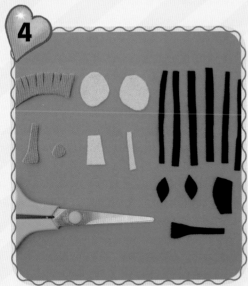

4

Cut out an elephant's ears, trunk,
and tail from blue felt. Cut out a
lion's mane, tail, and nose from
orange felt. Cut out a zebra's stripes,
mane, and tail from black felt.

Stick the felt shapes on to the
animals with fabric glue. Draw more
details on to the animals using a
black marker pen and finish them
off by sticking on googly eyes with
craft glue.

Paper Bouquet

For a special occasion, like a friend or relative's birthday, the Pretty Fabulous Friends know that they don't need money to give a beautiful bouquet of flowers. You probably have most of the things you need at home already and this bouquet is everlasting.

You will need:

- ★ Lettersize paper
- ★ Double-sided clear tape
- ★ Scissors
- ★ Black marker pen
- ★ Green garden canes

2

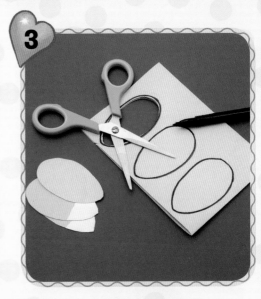

3

ut a strip of double-sided tape along both sides of the long edge of he paper. Don't remove the paper backing from the tape yet!

Fold the paper in half lengthwise so that the two strips of tape meet. Then fold it in half.

Draw three petal shapes on to the paper, making sure that one end of each petal is over the tape. Cut them out with scissors.

4

5

6

Peel off the paper from the tape on one petal. Stick the petal around the top of a green garden cane.

Repeat this, going around the cane until you have used all the petals.

Repeat steps 1 to 6 with different sheets of paper until you've made enough flowers for a bouquet! Peel back the petals to make the flowers look like they are in bloom.